Ireland's Wind of Change

Ireland's Wind of Change

Arjun Gambhir

Ireland's Wind of Change

First Published 01-06-2024

This book includes images created from Adobe Firefly under a premium subscription license. These images are used in compliance with the Adobe premium terms and conditions.

ISBN: 979-83-169-4990-8
Second Edition: April 6, 2025

Self-published by Nitin Gambhir

For permissions, inquiries, or additional information, please contact:
uno.nitin@gmail.com | A704 Saheta CGHS, Plot-30, Sector-4,Dwarka,Delhi 110075.

With clarity and insight, Gambhir discusses how wind, solar, and other green energy solutions could power Ireland's next generation, while addressing bureaucratic and infrastructural obstacles.

It's a compelling call for collaboration between government, business, and communities to transform Ireland into a leader in clean energy innovation.

Aligned to the UN Sustainable Development Goals

Introduction

As the winds of progress blow across the Emerald Isle, Ireland stands at a pivotal crossroads — one that challenges how we power our future, balance innovation with sustainability, and rethink what it truly means to lead in the age of climate urgency.

This book, *Ireland's Wind of Change*, is born out of curiosity, concern, and conviction. Written from the perspective of a young mind growing up in a rapidly changing world, it explores the intersection of technology, environmental responsibility, and policy. It is both a critique and a call to action, urging decision-makers, industries, and citizens alike to rethink the trajectory of energy in Ireland.

Over the past two decades, Ireland has made impressive strides in renewable energy, especially in wind generation. Yet, as data centers sprout across the nation, consuming massive amounts of electricity, the tension between digital growth and environmental responsibility grows sharper. Can Ireland meet its climate commitments while supporting a booming tech industry? Can policy, infrastructure, and innovation move fast enough to keep up with the climate clock?

These are the questions explored in the chapters ahead.

This is not just a story about kilowatts and climate targets. It's a reflection of youth perspective — passionate, hopeful, and unafraid to ask hard questions. Through facts, insights, and personal reflections, this book invites you to witness Ireland's energy transformation and imagine what's possible when ambition meets action.

Welcome to a journey of thought, purpose, and, hopefully, impact.

Arjun Gambhir
Dublin, Ireland

An old proverb "You can't clean a thing without making something else dirty" finds a new home in Ireland, a small country with small population and "thermo-stable" which led to the country becoming a strategic asset and a global leader in data-centre development in the last decade.

The country would miss its legally binding obligations of cutting emissions with data centers consumption crossing 20%.

In Ireland, the contribution of renewable electricity supply has grown from five percent to thirty nine percent since 2005. It provides several green energy options including solar, wind, geothermal, hydropower, biomass and tidal energy. These alternatives can significantly reduce the country's reliance on unsustainable energy sources.

Ireland is a global leader in onshore wind generation and together with solar, these sources represent mature technologies that Ireland has ample experience in connecting to the grid. Ireland must invest in more onshore renewable electricity generation, streamline processes, address the challenges faced in offshore wind development, increase interconnection, and incentivise electricity storage.

Solar is convenient and adaptable, perfectly suited to Ireland's green energy drive. The Irish government supports solar growth through the Climate Action Plan, providing grant and funding incentives and this makes solar energy an attractive option for Irish consumers.

Wind energy is another highly compatible green option for Ireland, accounting for approximately 86% of the country's renewable energy generation in 2023. Ireland holds the second-largest share of wind energy in the EU, behind Denmark.

To successfully achieve its goals, Ireland must invest in more onshore renewable electricity generation, streamline processes, address the challenges faced in offshore wind development, increase interconnection, and incentivise electricity storage.

By taking these measures, Ireland can demonstrate its commitment to its European targets and lead the way towards a greener, more sustainable future.

There exist widespread concerns about lengthy decision-making processes, often taking up to 90 weeks, due to coordination issues during planning. These planning process delays pose significant barriers to progress.

Ireland's planning and consenting system is operating at capacity and needs greater resourcing. Further scaling of wind energy is challenged by the nation's poorly interconnected electricity grid.

Data centres can make use of renewable sources like solar and wind-power energy to create an energy-supply profile that better fits customer demand.

During peak-demand periods when non-renewable sources are pricier, green energy can kick in. Surplus electricity generated from renewable sources can be stored or channelled back to the grid. Dispatchable technologies (e.g., batteries) can help data centres manage renewable energy supplies.

The integration of renewable energy in data centres can be achieved through various methods.

On-site renewable energy generation must be "dispatchable" i.e. capable of being turned on instantly when required which in a way adds limitations to use of Solar and Wind as sources.

Batteries, which most data centers already have can be used to store energy in case of a blackout.

These batteries can be charged using renewable power and then sent back to the grid when wind and solar generation is low, thus becoming Virtual Power Plants and part of the solution rather than the problem.

Off-site renewable energy procurement can source renewable energy from third-party suppliers who specialize in providing clean energy and enter into Power purchase agreements (PPAs) and renewable energy credits (RECs). Further, integrating energy storage solutions, such as batteries, allows data centers to store excess renewable energy for later use, ensuring a more consistent and reliable power supply.

Microgrids and decentralized energy systems help to implement the integration of renewable energy sources at a local level.

Stakeholders involved in the renewable energy industry widely noted that the Irish planning system continues to be a major. These planning process delays pose significant barriers to progress.

While there are ongoing challenges in the transition to renewable energy, a renewed commitment and collective effort can ensure Ireland maximises the environmental, economic, and social advantages from prioritising renewable energy development.

Policymakers must work with business to create investable markets and stimulate the right types of entrepreneurships. Ireland needs to look at more ambitious projects to generate renewables, particularly in relation to offshore wind.

Also, it needs to invest extensively in the local transmission and distribution network to support new forms of renewable power coming on stream.

It is crucial that all jurisdictions push to create investable markets to attract green money.

A key challenge in the global transition is stimulating the market for investable projects in regions with extensive fossil fuel legacy infrastructure and growing domestic energy demand.

To do this, the country needs to create an investable market for renewable energy.

Government should support the shift from brown to green through both incentives and disincentives. As we outlined above, they need to encourage the private sector to scale up the production of mature green technologies.

Financial institutions must do more to support transition and green innovation.

More funding needs to be directed toward green initiatives by the financial services sector. Financial institutions have a role to play in promoting demand and facilitating the supply of green money through new green finance products.

Working with government and regulators, they can identify policy and regulatory changes to enable financial product and service innovation, simplify guidelines, harmonize taxonomies.

Ireland must rise to the occasion, speed up its permitting and regulatory regimes and ensure energy generation solutions are available to facilitate the data centres.